W9-AHP-850

Pig Detectives

by Jenny Fretland VanVoorst

Consultant:
Bonnie V. Beaver
College of Veterinary Medicine
Texas A&M University

BEARPORT
PUBLISHING

Credits

Cover and Title Page, © Ursula Dueren/picture-alliance/dpa/AP Images; 4–5, © Robert Harding Picture Library/SuperStock; 6, 6–7, 8–9, © iStockphoto/Thinkstock; 10–11, © Biosphoto/SuperStock; 12–13, © Hemis.fr/SuperStock; 14–15, 16–17, © David Silverman/Getty Images; 18–19, © iStockphoto/Thinkstock; 20–21, © Robert Harding Picture Library/SuperStock; 22T, © Comstock/Thinkstock; 22B, 23T, 23B, © iStockphoto/Thinkstock.

Publisher: Kenn Goin
Senior Editor: Joyce Tavolacci
Creative Director: Spencer Brinker
Design: Craig Hinton
Photo Researcher: Arnold Ringstad

Library of Congress Cataloging-in-Publication Data

Fretland VanVoorst, Jenny, 1972–
  Pig Detectives / by Jenny Fretland VanVoorst.
    p. cm. — (We work!: Animals with jobs)
  Includes bibliographical references and index.
  ISBN 978-1-61772-899-0 (library binding) — ISBN 1-61772-899-3 (library binding)
 1. Swine—Juvenile literature. 2. Working animals—Juvenile literature. I. Title.
  SF395.5.F74 2014
  636.40886—dc23

                            2013011053

For more information, write to Bearport Publishing Company, Inc., 45 West 21st Street, Suite 3B, New York, New York 10010. Printed in the United States of America.

10 9 8 7 6 5 4 3 2 1

Contents

Jake the Pig Detective

Meet Jake the pig.

He works with a farmer to find a food called **truffles**.

How does Jake help out?

He puts his powerful nose to work.

farmer

Jake

The Nose Knows

Pigs have a great sense of smell.

Using their **snouts**, they pick up many smells that people cannot.

In fact, they can smell things buried 25 feet (7.6 m) underground!

snout

Hidden Truffles

A truffle is a round **fungus** that grows in soil near trees.

People love truffles for their special flavor.

truffles

Follow the Nose

Pigs do not need to be trained to find truffles.

They seek them out on their own.

Why?

Truffles give off a smell that pigs cannot resist.

Farmers bring pigs to areas where truffles might be growing.

Then the farmers let the pigs sniff the ground.

However, truffles are hard to find.

That is why farmers need special curly-tailed helpers!

pig sniffing for truffles

11

Digging Up Truffles

When pigs smell truffles, they stand still.

This tells the farmers, "We have found truffles!"

Then the pigs begin to dig up the special food.

pig standing still

However, the farmers must watch the pigs closely.

If they do not, the pigs will eat the tasty truffles!

A Risky Job

Some pigs help people with a different kind of job.

They search for buried bombs called **land mines**.

The pigs must be trained to do this risky job.

At first, pigs are taught to find fake mines.

After much practice, pigs are ready to find real mines.

14

a pig practicing sniffing for land mines

Finding Mines

When they find a mine, pigs stop digging and look up.

If they tried to dig up the mine, it could blow up.

Once the pigs find a mine, people safely dig it up.

That way, no one gets hurt.

pig looking
up

Smart as a Pig

It is easy to train pigs to find mines because they are very smart.

In fact, pigs are some of the smartest animals in the world.

Some experts think only apes, dolphins, and elephants are smarter.

On the Job

Pigs might be the best animal detectives in the business.

Some people think that pigs have a better sense of smell than dogs.

When people need help finding things, it is good to have a pig on the job!

Glossary

fungus (FUHN-gus) a group of living things that includes molds and mushrooms

land mines (LAND mynes) bombs that are buried underground

snouts (SNOUTS) the long, front parts of animals' heads, including the nose and usually the jaws and mouth

truffles (TRUFF-uhlz) rare mushrooms that grow underground

Index

Read More

Macken, JoAnn Early. *Pigs (Animals That Live on the Farm)*. Milwaukee, WI: Weekly Reader (2009).

Murray, Julie. *Crime-Fighting Animals (Going to Work)*. Edina, MN: ABDO (2009).

Learn More Online

To learn more about pig detectives, visit
www.bearportpublishing.com/WeWork

About the Author

Jenny Fretland VanVoorst is a writer and an editor of books for young people. She enjoys learning about all kinds of topics. When she is not reading and writing, Jenny enjoys kayaking, playing the piano, and watching wildlife. She lives in Minneapolis, Minnesota, with her husband, Brian, and their two pets.